The Last Laugh

Poems By
April Bulmer

Copyright © 2024 by April Bulmer

All rights reserved

No part of this book may be reproduced, stored in a retrieval system, or transmitted by any means, electronic, mechanical, photocopying, recording, or otherwise, without written permission from the author or publisher. There is one exception. Brief passages may be quoted in articles or reviews.

ISBN 978-1-55483-567-6 (trpb)
ISBN 978-1-55483-568-3 (e-book)

For My Funny Valentine

Introduction

"The Last Laugh" is a short book devoted to the art of clowning, a tradition that dates back to ancient Egypt, around the year 2500 BCE. There, the paradoxical relationship between the sacred and profane was resolved through the activities of the clown who was also regarded as a priest. He was described by the Pharoah as a divine spirit whose role was to delight the heart. The clown also created checks and balances by challenging the absolute authority of the ruler. The fool spoke what others dared not. These instincts are also grounded in many old and basic customs in other cultures. Historically, clowns undermined sacramental traditions with anarchy, discord and iconoclasm and restitched the fabric of religion and politics. For many societies embraced hierarchy, homogeneity and perfectionism – ideals that weakened them. Clowns worked against these tendencies.

    Each piece in this collection is narrated by a clown. Unique photographs accompany the poems.

It is my hope that readers regard mimes, jesters, jokers and fools as vital players in the history of Western theatre, as well as independent characters who, like Christ, continue to challenge the status quo and embroider the cultural cloth of the globe.

1.

I am a marionette.
I move with rhythm.
I perform great feats without a net.
I am not a man, descendent of Adam.
I am a circus clown,
puppet of heaven.

2.

It is the 5th dynasty of ancient Egypt.
I am an African Pygmy
known as a Danga in the courts.
My role is to amuse Pharoah
and members of the royal family.
You might call me a clown.

I dress in leopard skins and strange masks.
I dance and imitate gods.
For Egyptians enjoy impressions and comedy.

Priests also perform this function:
The rigid relationship
between the sacred and profane softens.

Whether ridiculing a king
or making him laugh at himself
the clown is a counterweight to authority.

Juggling is also prominent in Egyptian culture.
It is seen as meditative and a form of magic.
Some hieroglyphs feature juggling.
The trick known as cups and balls
is also sketched on walls.

3.

I am Venus, goddess of love and beauty.
Jupiter and Mars mock me.

4.

I am a clown, a buffoon in medieval Europe.
It is 1432, I play a key role in a Feast of Fools.
It takes place at the turn of the new year.
Lay people like me and lower clergy
improvise sermons and prayers.
We make fun of Christian scripture.

**

A few years later,
the church is fussy about its image
and popes see themselves as secular leaders.
We are rejected for our foolery and stabs.

**

In 1444, the theological faculty
at the University of Paris
sends a letter to all French bishops.
They hate the clowns and masqueraders
who are disguised as women, lions and mummers.
They curse our "indecent songs," our forms of dance.
They reject fools who eat greasy foods at the altar.

We are unwelcome in the house of God.
We are unsupervised and wild.
Religious leaders take legal action
and ban our shows.
We are booted from the church.
We wave goodbye without a smile.

5.

It is the Renaissance,
I am a clown in the Commedia Dell'Arte,
a woman applauded for my wit and craft.

First an itinerant street theatre,
we now perform indoors.
We are celebrated throughout Europe.
We are highly polished, we gleam.

We form guilds
and create contracts with new patrons.
We break from the ropes
that bind us to power centres
like church and state.

All of the clowns in the Commedia
are free agents now,
our livelihood dependent on our public appeal.
Our stock characters delight, shock and amaze.

**

It is 1697, we are expelled from Paris
for insulting the King's mistress.
The church rejects our plays as obscene.
It implies the presence of women is unholy,
declares our troupe blasphemes.

**

Today I am Zoe.
I reincarnated as a clown.
I work the streets of Montreal.

6.

I am a clown in a Pueblo tribe
of New Mexico called the Hopi.
My role is to ridicule serious ceremonies,
including harvest, marriage and death.
I wear white paint and tattered clothes.
Sometimes I sport wild colours and a mud mask.

My behaviour interrupts the order of ritual.
I parody solemn rites and dances
while the tribe marks traditional occasions.
I garble my speech or song,
turn sacred tongue into babble.

My tribe becomes less rigid
and frightened of change.
It celebrates my ways.

7.

My family and I are atheists.
I make fun of the Catholic Church.
I perform masses, marriages and baptisms.
Funerals too.
I am a clown in the pulpit.
I preach wit.

I reach deep and question my role.
Can I make jokes when families mourn?
Can I laugh at the dead,
pull flowers from their ears?
Sure, the church is a farce,
my miracles are real.

8.

White bucks and pink Cadillac.
Sexy chicks in the back seat.
I am patron saint of New Jersey.
Crowds genuflect to me.

9.

I am a clown.
I am a priest.
I am a prophet
and flop.
It is kingdom come.
I am alone.
Still masquerade as hobo.

10.

COVID-19 is a demon.
I am an exorcist.
I will vanquish him like a priest.

Granny waves from a distance at me.
Flowers bloom from my sleeve.
I will toss them to her
like a bride her bouquet,
bless Granny with laughter.
Later, we'll pray.

11.

I wear my wig to chapel.
La Belle Soeur dons her wimple.
We pray for Mother Superior
down in the dumps.

We appeal to a trinity
of Christ, Clown and Nun.

12.

I joined the circus in 1927.
I was but a boy.
I am a small man today
with the strength of a giant.
I pray to Louis Cyr,
l'homme le plus fort du monde.

13.

A hundred years ago,
audience members were farmers and labourers.
They appreciated physical tricks and acrobatics.

My grandfather, my father,
my aunts, uncles and I
were foot jugglers.
It was in our blood.
We were circus royalty.

I practised
and rose to the occasion.
I rarely dropped a prop.
I was Lord of the rings.

I paid my dues,
advanced to clown.
Am proud to wear the shoes.

14.

After the show
I phone my mom.
She was a clown
in Cirque du Soleil.
I was born on the road.
She held me as a child.
I loved to tweak her nose.

15.

I balance on an elephant.
A clown curtsies
beneath his great trunk.
Ringmaster takes a photo.
I will send it to Mother
ill in the hospital.

16.

I dream of the big top
and other circus clowns.
But when I wake
I am alone
save for my horse and wagon.

I rest in a small tent
on the prairie.
It is my home.
Only the wind applauds
my pratfall and poem.

17.

My mind is a cage:
Thoughts fly from a little door.
Doctor says I am mentally ill:
An empty clown.
For silence haunts like birdsong.

18.

I am discombobulated.
I have lost my mind.
My heart is divorced
from my head.
Still, I stand tall in my shoes.
My body is a sleight of hand.

19.

I am a sad clown.
I toke pot.
The smoke hangs
in the air like an acrobat.

20.

My makeup smears when I cry.
I place a tear in my pocket.
It waters the flowers I hide.
They bloom in polka dots
and laughter.

21.

I am a street clown.
How tired I am.
I rest on a bench
before a store.
It sells old records and books.
People pass me,
think I beg,
turn tricks for sex.
I make my way
with a bag of balloons
heavy with magic.

22.

I am a poet.
My typewriter is red.
My suit and hat too.
But, Baby, my poems
my poems sing the blues.

23.

I am Claudette, a clown's wife.
He mimes, makes signs.
I wash his smile, his frown each night.
They stain my hands.
I bear the weight of quiet.

24.

I put my foot down.
I know my own mind.
I am the clown in the family.
I speak truth in pantomime.

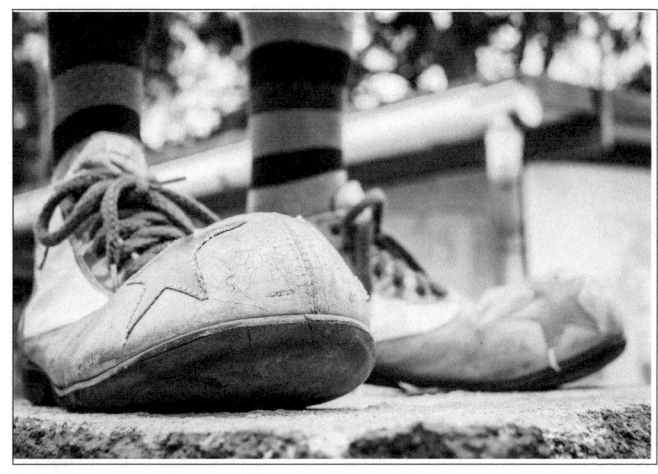

25.

I hold my father's pocket watches.
I love their steady tick.
I joined the circus
like Dad.
I catch glimpses of his spirit,
elusive as time.
He is sudden and gone
like the wave of a mime.

26.

Mother, you called me a dreamer
as I pumped my arms
like Arnold Schwarzenegger.

Today I am a lion tamer.
I am a clown.
I am Christ,
bear the weight of the world.

27.

We arrive in Spain
at high noon.
The roadies get to work.
Some clowns rest.
I slow my pace.
Today I moisturize.
Tomorrow I will paint my face.

28.

I love a clown.
I paint my face for him.

Angels gather to bless us.
The circus whispers:
Jealous.

I dance beneath the stars.
Silly Billy sings to the universe.

29.

I wait for my love,
I wipe the steam from my glass.
I will press my nose
to the window
like a hound.
I imagine Howie's face
a masterpiece
framed in the pane:
My beautiful clown.

30.

I press my face to your windowpane.
"Can you see me wave?
Hello, Clown. How are you today?"

31.

Howie leaves a gift:
A picture frame
and a card:
You, too, are beautiful
may you hang in the Louvre.

32.

I wear a little hat.
A daisy blooms from the brim.
I am a sexy clown
and attract pretty women.
I swing with Trixie
on the flying trapeze,
an acrobat who contorts for me.

33.

Polka Dot wears many faces
and comical hats.
Plays kazoo,
poses as a prat.

Some days, he babbles
like King Lear's fool.
Still, all the world loves a clown.

He is a tightrope walker too.
His careful feet
gloved in slippers
leave footprints on the sky.
He balances, like Christ,
without a net.

34.

Clown, today we wed.
My heart blooms for you.
It is soft and red
like a beautiful balloon.

35.

Acknowledgments

The photo depicting the cover is called Clown Posing with Dog Dressed in Clown Costume by Everett Collection. See shutterstock.com.

The photo depicting the dedication is called Heart Shape Balloon in the Forest by Sovastock. See shutterstock.com.

The photo depicting the introduction is called Clown Christ Renaissance Painting by Sophie Aurora. See creativefabrica.com.

The photo depicting Poem 1 is called Actor as a Marionette by RossHelen. See Shutterstock.com.

The photo depicting Poem 2 is called Ancient Egyptian Clown by nightmare fuel. See deviantart.com.

The photo depicting Poem 3 is called Greek Goddess with Clown Nose by iambada. See istockphoto.com.

The photo depicting Poem 4 is called Stone Jester by Marbury. See istockphoto.com.

The photo depicting Poem 5 is called Probeert Harlekijn by Art World. See alamy.com.

The photo depicting Poem 6 is called 1930s Head Clown Cochare Koshare in Costume Makeup San Ildefonso Pueblo New Mexico by ClassicStock. See alamy.com.

The photo depicting Poem 7 is called Clown Isolated Silhoutte by WujuPlantet. See shutterstock.com.

The photo depicting Poem 8 is called Parade with a Convertible in New Jersey, USA Stock Photo by atlantic kid. See istockphoto.com.

The photo depicting Poem 9 is called Being a Joker is No Picnic Studio Shot by Antoniy Karpenko. See shutterstock.com.

The photo depicting Poem 10 is called Mattie the Clown of Clowns International Preparing to elebrate the 75th Anniversary of Grimaldi Clown Service on Sunday 7th February 2021, London, UK by Jeff Gilbert. See alamy.com.

The photo depicting Poem 11 is called Nun with Clown by Erickson Stock. See alamy.com.

The photo depicting Poem 12 is called Circus Performer Pulling Horse's Tail by Everett Collection. See Shutterstock.com.

The photo depicting Poem 13 is called If Attacked by Clowns, Go For the Juggler First Humorous Sign at Auto Repair Shop. St Paul Minnesota MN USA by Steve Skjold. See alamy.com.

The photo depicting Poem 14 is called Crazy Scary Clown Stock Photo by knape. See istockphoto.com.

The photo depicting Poem 15 is called Clowning Around by Everett Collection. See everettcollection.com.

The photo depicting Poem 16 is called Medieval Scene with Horse by Runa0410. See Shutterstock.com.

The photo depicting Poem 17 is called Illustration of Man With Open Birdcage Over His Head, Surreal Freedom Concept by fran_kie. See Shutterstock.com.

The photo depicting Poem 18 is called Illustration of Creepy Clown Performance Holding His Head with Hand; Horror Humor Concept by fran_kie. See Shutterstock.com.

The photo depicting Poem 19 is called Crazy Scary Clown Stock Photo by knape. See istockphoto.com.

The photo depicting Poem 20 is called Dramatic Vertical Portrait of Female Mime Artist by SeventyFour. See Shutterstock.com.

The photo depicting Poem 21 is called Clown Sitting in Front of Antique Bookstore Stock Photo by Bratislav Stefonovic. See istockphoto.com.

The photo depicting Poem 22 is called Mime in a Red Suit Prints on a Typewriter Stock Photo by JohnAlexandr. See istockphoto.com.

The photo depicting Poem 23 is called Portrait of a Male Mime Artist Standing Under Umbrella Expressing Sadness and Loneliness. Love. Grunge Background by Kiselev Andrey Valerevich. See shutterstock.com.

The photo depicting Poem 24 is called Black and White Clown Shoes by Caterina Moranti. See Shutterstock.com.

The photo depicting Poem 25 is called Man and Time Stock Photo by suricoma. See istockphoto.com.

The photo depicting Poem 26 is called Black and White Portrait of Mime Actor Stock Photo by korionov. See istockphoto.com.

The photo depicting Poem 27 is called Barcelona –
Spain, 12.26.2012: Raluy Circus Ticket Office
During Their Stay in Barcelona by alexat25. See
istockphoto.com.

The photo depicting Poem 28 is called Portrait of a
Sad Mime Stock Photo by karionov. See
istockphoto.com.

The photo depicting Poem 29 is called Photo of
Russian Circus Clown by Stas Knyazev. See
shutterstock.com.

The photo depicting Poem 30 is called Face of
Mime Behind Glass with Multi-Colored Paint
Stains Stock Photo by korionov. See
istockphoto.com.

The photo depicting Poem 31 is called Photo of
Russian Circus Clown by Stas Knyazev. See
shutterstock.com.

The photo depicting Poem 32 is called Woman
Holding Trapeze Bar with Clown, Smiling Stock
Photo by Tom Kelley Archives. See
istockphoto.com.

The poem depicting Poem 33 is called A Tight Rope
Walker Hovers Above the Crowds During Stage 8
of the Tour de France, Oyonnax to Le Grand

Bornand by David Stockman/Pool/GodingImage. See alamy.com.

The photo depicting Poem 34 is called Cute Young Girl by ironika. See shutterstock.com.

The photo depicting Poem 35 is called Clown Makeup by Oilly. See shutterstock.com.

The photo depicting the acknowledgments is called Clown with White Painted Face, Red Nose, Wearing a Hat and Carrying a Suitcase in the Guildhall Square, Derry, Londonderry, Nort by George Sweeney. See alamy.com.

The photo depicting the bibliography is called Christmas Parade Stock Photo by PeteMuller. See istock.com.

The photo depicting the biography is called Circus Clown, Gary Brophy of the Sunrise Circus by Rob Walls. See alamy.com.

The photo depicting the back cover blurb is called Clowns, Punch and Judy Men/Women Plus May 2000 Methodist Minister Ken Elworthy [L] at a Service at St. Paul's Church in Covent Garden for the Mayfair Which Falls on Punch's 338 Birthday by Tom Pilston. See alamy.com.

Bibliography

LeBank, Ezra and Bridel, David. *Clowns: In Conversation Second Edition*. London and New York: Routledge Taylor and Francis Group, 2023.

"A Brief Walk Through Clown History [Part One]." Clown Antics, https://www.clownantics.com/blogs/clownantics-blog/a-brief-walk-through-clown-history-part-one September 21, 2018.

Biography

April Bulmer is a Canadian poet. She holds Master's degrees in creative writing, religion and theological studies from major universities. She also holds an Honours B.A. in mass communications and studied dance, music and art history. Much of her writing deals with women and spirituality and the divine feminine. Many of her dozen books have been shortlisted for awards, including the International Beverly Prize for Literature in London, England, the Pat Lowther Memorial Award for the best book of poetry by a Canadian woman, the Next Generation Indie Book Awards in the U.S and the Global Book Awards. She won the YWCA Women of Distinction Award in the art and culture category in Cambridge, Ontario where she lives. April's work has also been celebrated and published widely in prestigious journals, anthologies and newspapers. To contact April Bulmer email april.poet@bell.net.

For critical response to April's writing and more biographical information, please see: www.aprilbulmer.wordpress.com.
To purchase her books, please see: www.aprilbulmer.com.

Made in the USA
Monee, IL
04 May 2026

49445475R10033